Celebrations in My World

S0-AWH-197

PASSOVER

Molly
Aloian

Crabtree Publishing Company

www.crabtreebooks.com

Crabtree Publishing Company

www.crabtreebooks.com

Author: Molly Aloian
Coordinating editor: Chester Fisher
Series and project editor: Penny Dowdy
Editor: Adrianna Morganelli
Proofreader: Crystal Sikkens
Project editor: Robert Walker
Production coordinator: Katherine Berti
Prepress technician: Katherine Berti
Project manager: Kumar Kunal (Q2AMEDIA)
Art direction: Dibakar Acharjee (Q2AMEDIA)
Cover design: Tarang Saggar (Q2AMEDIA)
Design: Ritu Chopra (Q2AMEDIA)
Photo research: Farheen Aadil (Q2AMEDIA)

Photographs:
Alamy: Corbis Premium RF: p. 23; Israel images: p. 25;
    Jon Arnold Images Ltd.: p. 6; North Wind Picture Archives:
    p. 7, 11; PhotoStock-Israel: p. 14, 24; Helene Rogers: p. 18
Circa Art: p. 12
Corbis: Leland Bobbé: p. 1, 28; Annie Griffiths Belt: p. 30; Frans
    Lemmens/zefa: p. 10; Araldo de Luca: p. 9; Richard T. Nowitz:
    p. 26; Roger Ressmeyer: front cover, p. 17
Dreamstime: p. 4
Getty Images: Uriel Sinai/Stringer: p. 5
Jupiter Images: Comstock: p. 8; PNC: p. 29
Photolibrary: Richard T. Nowitz: p. 19
Reuters: Ronen Zvulun: p. 15
Shutterstock: Noam Armonn: p. 16; diligent: p. 21; Eugene Ivanov:
    front cover (star); Jasna: p. 22; Mikhail Levit: p. 20; Roman Sigaev:
    p. 13; Wil Tilroe-Otte: p. 31; Andrey Zyk: folio glyph
Stringer: Bill Pugliano: p. 27

Library and Archives Canada Cataloguing in Publication

Aloian, Molly
    Passover / Molly Aloian.

(Celebrations in my world)
Includes index.
ISBN 978-0-7787-4293-7 (bound).--ISBN 978-0-7787-4311-8 (pbk.)

    1. Passover--Juvenile literature. I. Title. II. Series: Celebrations
in my world

BM695.P3 A46 2009   j296.4'37   C2009-900232-9

Library of Congress Cataloging-in-Publication Data

Aloian, Molly.
    Passover / Molly Aloian.
        p. cm. -- (Celebrations in my world)
    Includes index.
    ISBN 978-0-7787-4311-8 (pbk. : alk. paper) -- ISBN 978-0-7787-4293-7
(reinforced library binding : alk. paper)
    1. Passover--Juvenile literature. I. Title. II. Series.

BM695.P3A385 2009
296.4'37--dc22

                                2009000328

Crabtree Publishing Company

www.crabtreebooks.com   1-800-387-7650

Published in Canada
Crabtree Publishing
616 Welland Ave.
St. Catharines, ON
L2M 5V6

Published in the United States
Crabtree Publishing
PMB16A
350 Fifth Ave., Suite 3308
New York, NY 10118

Published in the United Kingdom
Crabtree Publishing
White Cross Mills
High Town, Lancaster
LA1 4XS

Published in Australia
Crabtree Publishing
386 Mt. Alexander Rd.
Ascot Vale (Melbourne)
VIC 3032

Contents

What is Passover? 4

The Story of Passover 6

Moses 8

Ten Plagues 10

Free At Last 12

No Hametz 14

Seder 16

The Haggadah 18

A Special Table 20

Four Questions 22

Reciting the Plagues 24

Songs and Blessings 26

Finding the Afikomen 28

Peace on Earth 30

Glossary and Index 32

What is Passover?

Passover is a holiday that people of the Jewish religion celebrate. Jewish people live all over the world. No matter where they live, they celebrate Passover in March or April, during spring. The exact dates change from year to year.

Passover begins at sundown.

DID YOU KNOW?

*During Passover, people remember the **Exodus**, the story of how Jewish slaves in Egypt escaped to freedom.*

Many people come to Jerusalem, a city in Israel, to celebrate Passover.

Passover lasts for eight days. Many Jewish people celebrate Passover with their families and friends. The adults teach the children all about the holiday.

The Story of Passover

During the celebration, Jewish people remember the story of Passover. Thousands of years ago, a shortage of food caused the Jewish people to leave their homes in Israel and move to Egypt. The Egyptian **Pharaoh** made Jewish people **slaves**.

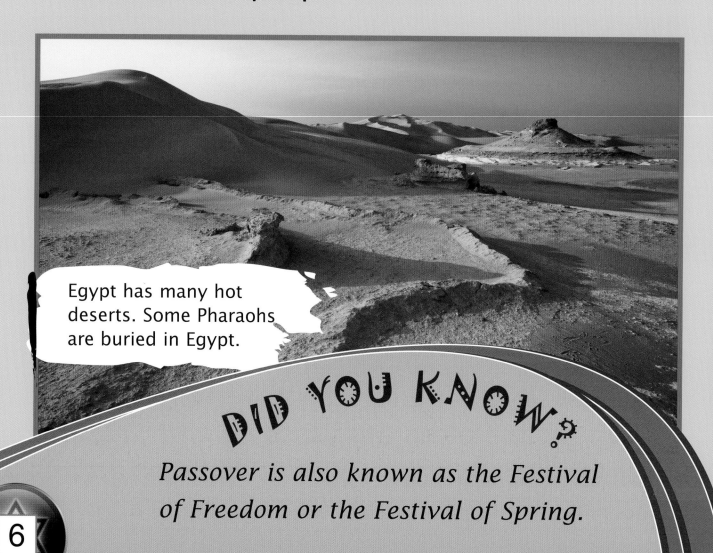

Egypt has many hot deserts. Some Pharaohs are buried in Egypt.

DID YOU KNOW?

Passover is also known as the Festival of Freedom or the Festival of Spring.

Day after day, the Jewish people were forced to work in the hot sun. They were slaves in Egypt for about 400 years. They wanted to escape from Egypt, but they did not know how to get away.

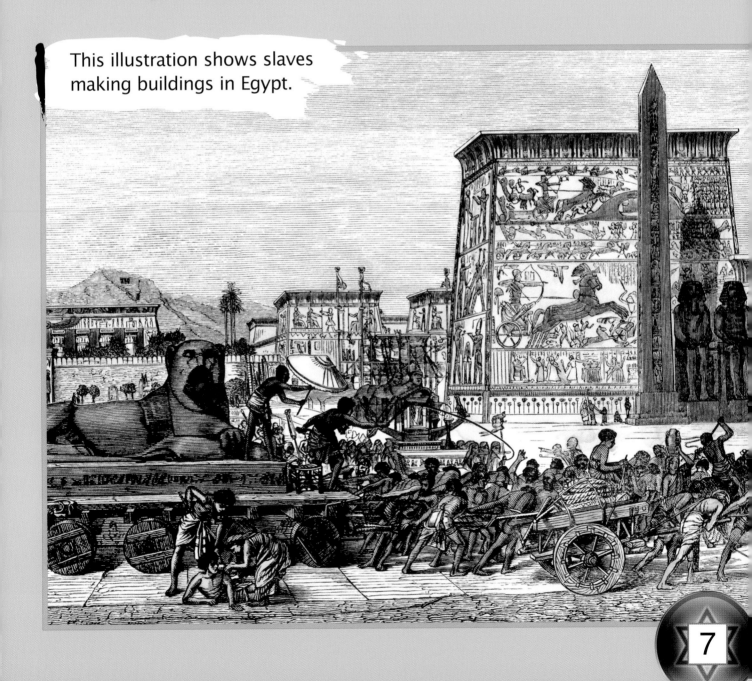

This illustration shows slaves making buildings in Egypt.

Moses

The Torah tells the stories of the ancient Jewish people. The Torah tells how God chose a brave man named Moses to help the slaves. Moses asked the Pharaoh to free the slaves and let them leave Egypt. The Pharaoh did not listen to Moses.

- The Torah is the most important writing in the Jewish religion.

DID YOU KNOW?

The Torah includes a story of Moses performing miracles.

Moses was not afraid of the Pharaoh. Moses warned the Pharaoh that God would punish him if he did not free the slaves. The Pharaoh still refused to let the slaves leave Egypt. Instead, he kept making them work very hard.

This sculpture of Moses was made over 500 years ago.

Ten Plagues

According to the Torah, God sent ten **plagues** to Egypt to punish the Pharaoh. With each plague, Moses asked the Pharaoh to let the slaves go. Each time the Pharaoh said no. All the fish in the Nile River died. **Hail** and fire fell from the sky. Frogs, locusts, and flies covered the land.

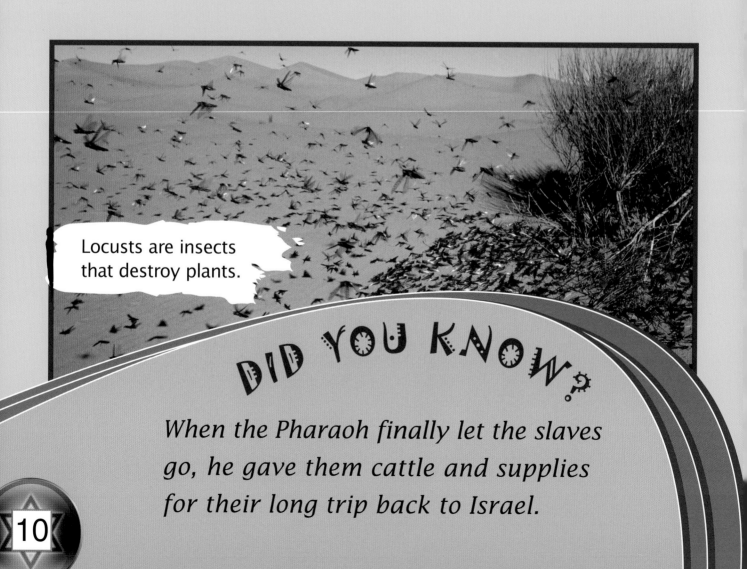

Locusts are insects that destroy plants.

DID YOU KNOW?

When the Pharaoh finally let the slaves go, he gave them cattle and supplies for their long trip back to Israel.

The last plague was the worst of all the ten plagues. The oldest son in every Egyptian family died. Even the Pharaoh's oldest son died. The Pharaoh finally let the Jewish people go.

Moses led the Jewish people out of Egypt.

Free At Last

The Jewish people collected their belongings and ran out of Egypt. They had to carry all their belongings on their backs. They were afraid the Pharaoh would change his mind, so they did not cook food before their trip.

This drawing shows the Jewish people crossing the Red Sea.

DID YOU KNOW?

Jewish stories tell how Moses parted the water of the Red Sea. The Jewish people could walk safely through the sea to the opposite shore.

• Matzah is a flat bread because it has no yeast.

They brought the bread dough they were preparing to bake. When the Jewish people were safely out of Egypt, they finally rested. They baked their bread in the hot desert sun. They had no **yeast** to make it rise, so the bread was flat. This flat bread was called matzah.

13

No Hametz

Jewish people eat matzah during Passover. During Passover, Jewish people do not eat any hametz, or breads that have yeast. So for eight days, they do not have cakes, rolls, or even a regular sandwich.

This boy and his father help people in need.

DID YOU KNOW?

During Passover, people think of those who do not have enough food to eat. Some people give food and money to people in need.

These children work hard making matzah.

Jewish people eat only matzah during Passover to remember what it was like for the Jewish people in Egypt. They try to imagine that they are the ones leaving Egypt. They also want to get rid of their own **pride** and "puffed up" thoughts.

15

Seder

On the first or second night of Passover, people gather together for a special feast called the Seder. They eat special foods including lamb, fish, stews, and chicken soup with matzah. Many people prepare the Seder foods using old family recipes.

● This woman is serving chicken soup with matzah balls at the Seder.

DID YOU KNOW?

Adults and children often cook foods together for the Seder. They may tell Passover stories as they prepare the foods.

People drink wine or juice during the Seder. They also pray, sing songs, and tell stories. They tell the story of Passover from long ago. They talk about the miracles that helped save the Jewish slaves.

This family is enjoying the Seder.

The Haggadah

During the Seder, people read from a very old book called the Haggadah. The word "Haggadah" means "telling" in Hebrew. The Haggadah contains prayers, stories, and songs. It tells the Exodus story of how the slaves left Egypt.

THE PASSOVER HAGGADAH
ILLUSTRATED BY HEINZ SEELIG

• This Haggadah has beautiful illustrations.

DID YOU KNOW?

It is important for each generation to pass down the Exodus story to the next generation.

18

This family reads from the Haggadah at a Passover Seder.

There are also beautiful illustrations in the Haggadah. Jewish people all over the world **cherish** the Haggadah because it is a very special book. The first printed version was published more than 500 years ago.

A Special Table

Many Jewish people have special dishes and glasses that are used only for their Passover celebrations. Some people use special silver candlesticks. They may also use **engraved** wine goblets called Passover Kiddush cups.

The engraved Kiddush cup is only used for Passover.

DID YOU KNOW?

The foods on the Seder plate are always placed in the order that they are eaten.

People place a Seder plate at the center of the table. A Seder plate usually includes an egg, lettuce or celery, a lamb bone, horseradish or other bitter herbs, parsley or a potato, and haroset. Haroset is a mixture of fruit, nuts, and wine. These are symbols of Passover.

● This picture shows a Seder plate.

Four Questions

During the Seder, the youngest child sings a chant called the "Four Questions." "Why on this night do we eat only matzah?" The matzah reminds them of the food the escaping slaves ate. "Why on this night do we eat especially bitter herbs?" The bitter herbs represent the Pharaoh's cruelty.

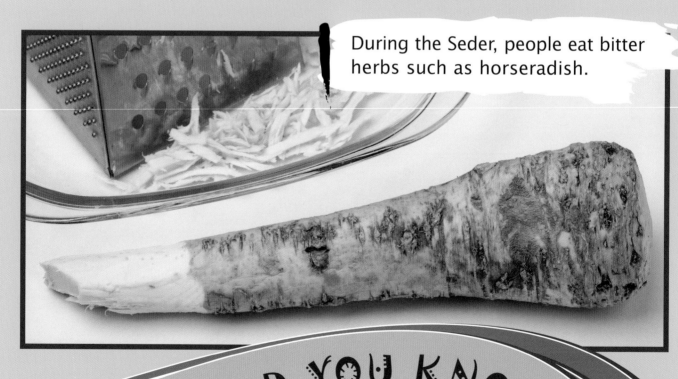

During the Seder, people eat bitter herbs such as horseradish.

DID YOU KNOW?

Each food in the Seder meal helps children understand the answers to the "Four Questions."

"Why on this night do we dip the herbs twice?" The first dip reminds us of the slaves' hard work. The second dip is salty, like the slaves' tears. "Why on this night do we eat in a reclining position?" The Jewish people are now free and can relax.

This girl is chanting the "Four Questions" as her family reads along in the Haggadah.

Reciting the Plagues

People recite, or list, the plagues at the Seder. Some families just recite the stories. Others act them out or sing songs for each plague. They wear costumes and use props to make the stories meaningful.

● People of all ages recite the plagues during the Seder.

The stories at the Seder meal help people remember. The Haggadah explains that the people at the Seder meal should feel that they have been through the Exodus, too.

Each time one of the plagues is mentioned, everyone dips their finger in wine and pours out a drop.

25

Songs and Blessings

People sing and pray during the Seder. The songs are ones of **praise** and **faith** from the Haggadah. People sing songs before and after the Seder. They say special prayers before and after the Seder, as well.

These children are acting out the story of Exodus.

DID YOU KNOW?

Children sometimes act out the story of Exodus at the Passover table.

This family is saying a prayer.

People also pray for others who are suffering or who are in need. Passover is a celebration, but it is also a serious time. It is important for people to remember that their ancestors were slaves. The Jewish slaves suffered, just as some people do today.

Finding the Afikomen

The last thing people eat during the Seder is the broken piece of matzah called the afikomen. An adult might hide the afikomen while the children are not looking. The children search to find it!

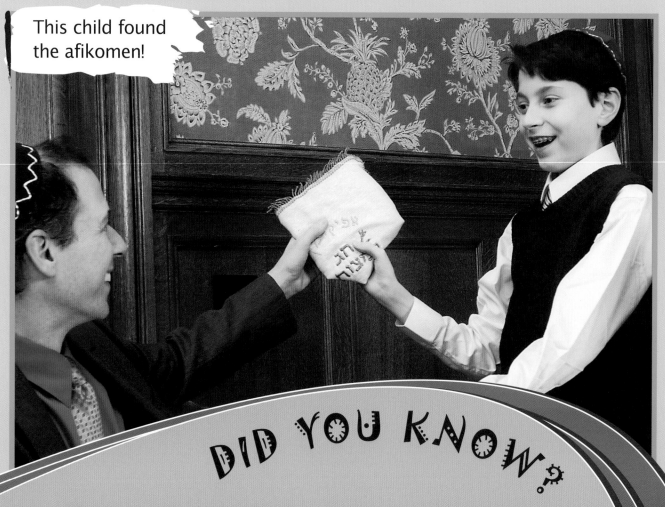

This child found the afikomen!

DID YOU KNOW?

The Haggadah begins at the back. People read the pages of the Haggadah from right to left.

Children might also steal the afikomen. They demand a **ransom** before giving the afikomen back.

Everyone eats a bit of the afikomen. Then the Seder meal is finished. The child who found or stole the afikomen gets a present. This reward reminds the children of the reward the Jewish slaves received for trusting God— their freedom!

● This boy found the afikomen and got a present.

29

Peace on Earth

The Haggadah says that one day, a man named Elijah will come and bring peace on Earth. People open a door for Elijah in the hopes that he will soon arrive. An extra seat is set at the Seder table to show that Elijah is welcome.

- This door is left open for Elijah.

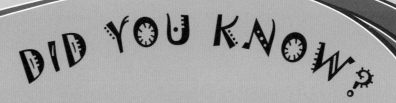

Celebrating Passover helps children learn the importance of freedom for all people.

The members of this family realize that there is nothing as good as being free!

The eight days of Passover are the most important holidays for Jewish people. They remember how important their freedom is. Passover is also a time to think of others. Prayers and songs teach children to take care of people in need.

Glossary

cherish To value or treasure something

engraved When something has letters or designs cut or carved into it

Exodus The second book of the Torah

faith A belief in something

hail Small lumps of ice that fall from clouds

Pharaoh A ruler of ancient Egypt

plague A disaster that harms many people

praise To admire or honor

pride The high opinion of yourself

ransom Something paid for the freedom of a captured thing

slave A person who is forced to work without pay

yeast A substance that makes bread rise

Index

afikomen 28, 29

Egypt 4, 6, 7, 8, 9, 10, 11, 12, 13, 15, 18

Elijah 30

Exodus 4, 18, 25, 26

foods 12, 14, 16, 20, 22

Four Questions 22, 23

freedom 4, 6, 29, 30, 31

Haggadah 18–19, 25, 26, 28, 30

hametz 14

herbs 21, 22, 23

Kiddush cups 20

matzah 13, 14, 15, 16, 22, 28

Moses 8, 9, 10, 11, 12

peace 30

Pharaoh 6, 8, 9, 10, 11, 12, 22

plagues 10, 11, 24

prayers 18, 26, 27, 31

Seder 16–17, 20, 21, 22, 24, 25, 26, 28, 29, 30

slaves 4, 6, 7, 8, 9, 10, 12, 17, 18, 22, 23, 24, 27, 29

stories 4, 6, 8, 12, 16, 17, 18, 24, 25

Torah 8, 10

Printed in the U.S.A.—CG